STUDY GUIDE

Learning to Love the Psalms

W. Robert Godfrey

LIGONIER MINISTRIES

Renew your Mind.

LIGONIER.ORG | 800-435-4343

Copyright © 2017 Ligonier Ministries
421 Ligonier Court, Sanford, FL 32771
E-mail: info@ligonier.org
All rights reserved.
No reproduction of this work without permission.
Printed in the United States of America.

1

Introduction (Part 1): Attractions & Difficulties

INTRODUCTION

The Psalms have a Godward direction, being God's words to us to give back to Him. In this lesson, Dr. Godfrey discusses the uniqueness of the Psalms as well as the difficulties that must be overcome if we are to learn to love them.

LESSON OBJECTIVES

1. To highlight the unique place of the Psalms in the Christian life
2. To introduce the five difficulties we have when reading the Psalms
3. To address the first difficulty by showing how the Psalms are structured

SCRIPTURE READING

Blessed is the man who walks not in the counsel of the wicked, nor stands in the way of sinners, nor sits in the seat of scoffers; but his delight is in the law of the Lord, and on his law he meditates day and night.

—Psalm 1:1–2

LECTURE OUTLINE

A. This series is titled *Learning to Love the Psalms* because Christians today have become increasingly detached from the Psalms despite their attractions.

1. The Psalms have been a tremendous comfort to God's people historically and remain something with which we can richly connect.
2. The poetic nature of the Psalms continually unveils things previously unseen every time we read them.
3. The Godward direction of the Psalms make them uniquely helpful; they are God's inspired words to us to give back to Him.

4. The Psalms are a rich resource for the Christian life, but they present some challenges worth overcoming so that we might learn to love them more.

B. The Psalms present a challenge to us because of five main difficulties.
  1. The Psalms are a collection of 150 poems that at a glance do not appear to be organized, which makes it difficult to interpret in terms of the whole book.
  2. The Psalms have a poetic literary form that requires us to slow down and meditate on them, contrary to our fast-paced, non-poetic age.
  3. The Psalms require that we understand who is speaking to us in them.
      a. The Psalms are God's words to us to speak back to Him, but they must be understood within the appropriate context.
      b. Psalms like the imprecatory psalms make it difficult for Christians to understand how they relate to the context of the New Testament.
  4. The Psalms must be read with an understanding of the relationship between the Old Testament and the New Testament in order to see their relevance.
  5. The Psalms are difficult to outline.
      a. Some books of the Bible have a clear outline, but the Psalms are difficult to outline even when considered individually.
      b. Psalm 95 is an example of how an individual psalm can shift thematically from a call to worship to a solemn and severe warning.

C. The Psalms are divided into five books with a clear movement and destination.
  1. The title of the Psalms when translated from the Hebrew is *The Book of Praises*, and the book has always been divided into five parts.
      a. The title of the Psalms should inform us of its movement as a whole, even though there are different genres of psalms.
      b. The organization and movement of the Psalms is further seen in the progression of its fivefold division.
  2. Book One can be titled "Confidence in God's Care."
      a. The psalms in Book One tend to be personal, reflecting some level of distress that quickly resolves into confidence in God.
      b. They are where you should look for comfort in distress, being psalms for those who are oppressed, sick, or suffering.
  3. Book Two can be titled "Commitment to God's Kingdom."
      a. The psalms in Book Two are less personal but more community oriented.
      b. They take into consideration the whole people of God and how God is providing for His people.
  4. Book Three can be titled "Crisis Over God's Promises."
      a. The psalms in Book Three are the emotional heart of the Psalms, containing the most distressful psalms in the Psalter.
      b. They represent a great crisis in the life of the psalmist, a spiritual crisis of doubt and disillusion in the promises of God.

5. Book Four can be titled "Comfort in God's Faithfulness."
   a. The psalms in Book Four reflect on God's work in creation and His covenant with Abraham.
   b. They set out to answer the cry of the psalmist in Book Three by proving that God is faithful to His promises.
6. Book Five can be titled "Celebration of God's Salvation."
   a. The psalms in Book Five are a review of Israel's history and show that God has had a plan throughout the history of Israel, even amidst exile.
   b. They further prove that God is a promise-keeping God and culminate in psalms of praise toward the end of the book.
7. The structure of the Psalms demonstrates that it is a cohesive collection of 150 poems that have not been put together randomly.
   a. Psalms 1 and 2 serve as personal and cosmic introductions to the book, respectively, and the psalms of praise in Book Five are its conclusion.
   b. The movement of the Psalms mirrors the lives and experiences of the people of God, giving us the language to pray to God when in crisis and reminding us of His faithfulness so that we might praise Him.

STUDY QUESTIONS

1. Slowing down to meditate on the structure of the Psalms is difficult because of the age in which we live.
   a. True
   b. False

2. Why should Psalms be considered a unique book of the Bible?
   a. Because of their poetic literary form
   b. Because of their Godward direction
   c. Because of their structural cohesion
   d. Because of their apparent difficulty

3. The spiritual distress found in Book Three of the Psalms is a result of doubting which of God's qualities?
   a. His goodness
   b. His sovereignty
   c. His promises
   d. His power

4. Book Five is the emotional heart of the Psalms because it is the longest book of the Psalms.
   a. True
   b. False

5   In which book of the Psalms are the psalms characteristically less personal and more community oriented?
    a.   Book One: Confidence in God's Care
    b.   Book Two: Commitment to God's Kingdom
    c.   Book Three: Crisis of God's People
    d.   Book Five: Celebration of God's Salvation

6.   What is challenging about the fact that the Psalms are a collection of 150 poems?
    a.   It becomes difficult to see the relevance of the Psalms.
    b.   It becomes difficult to see the profundity of the Psalms.
    c.   It becomes difficult to see the wholeness of the Psalms.
    d.   It becomes difficult to see the perspective of the Psalms.

DISCUSSION QUESTIONS

1.   What are some of the reasons Dr. Godfrey titled this series *Learning to Love the Psalms*?

2.   Why are the Psalms uniquely helpful in the Christian life and how do they progress in a way that mirrors our lives and experiences? Describe a time in your life when the Psalms were a great comfort to you in time of need.

3.   What would be some benefits to memorizing the titles Dr. Godfrey gave to each book of the Psalms?

4.   In what ways should the Psalms inform and embolden our prayers? How would the content of our prayers be deprived without them?

2

Introduction (Part 2): Solving Difficulties

INTRODUCTION

Learning to love the Psalms requires us to overcome the interpretive difficulties outlined in the previous lecture. In this lesson, Dr. Godfrey demonstrates how the difficulties commonly perceived in the Psalms are not that difficult after all.

LESSON OBJECTIVES

1. To simplify the difficulties of poetry and perspective in the Psalms
2. To explain how the Old and New Testament relate in the Psalms
3. To showcase the overarching themes of the Psalms

SCRIPTURE READING

Why do the nations rage and the peoples plot in vain?

—Psalm 2:1

Kiss the Son, lest he be angry, and you perish in the way, for his wrath is quickly kindled. Blessed are all who take refuge in him.

—Psalm 2:12

LECTURE OUTLINE

A. The literary form of the Psalms presents us with a difficulty that must be overcome in order for us to grow in our love for the Psalms.

   1. Poetry is a powerful literary tool that can deepen our appreciation for the Word of God by slowing us down to meditate on it.

      a. Poetry is a literary device that has the potential to make powerful truths even more powerful through its expressive character.

      b. Psalm 23 expresses the powerful truth of God's provisional character in the poetic and memorable expression, "The Lord is my shepherd."

  2. Poetry requires meditation to understand its rich meaning.

      a. The Hebrew word for "meditation" could be translated as "mutter," giving one the sense of reflective and repetitious reading.

      b. Hebrew poetry helps us to meditate by being repetitious, as can be seen in the parallel structure of Psalm 1.

  3. Hebrew poetry places emphasis on the meaning of a poem by placing its most important part at the center of the poem.

      a. English is markedly different from Hebrew in its emphasis on the end of a text as opposed to the center of a text.

      b. The shift in Psalm 23 from a shepherd's care to a king's feast seems unrelated, but the imagery is held together by the center of the psalm, "For you are with me" (v. 4).

B. Our understanding of the voice speaking to us in the Psalms presents us with a difficulty that must be overcome in order to grow in our love for the Psalms.

  1. The primary person who speaks to us in the Psalms is the king of God's people, so all of the psalms should be seen as royal psalms.

      a. The Bible looks at the whole collection of psalms, whether written by David or not, as Davidic psalms; they are psalms of the king.

      b. David, as king, speaks both personally and communally in the psalms such that we are able to identify his history as our history.

  2. Understanding the psalms as royal psalms of David helps us to see their function as psalms of Jesus Christ, the King of kings and Lord of lords.

      a. Jesus is David's greater Son, so whatever is spoken of as true of David as king is profoundly true of Jesus as King.

      b. Jesus used Psalm 110 to confound the Pharisees, showing Himself to be God's Son, who is simultaneously David's Son and David's Lord.

      c. The psalms not only speak of Christ, they are also spoken by Christ, quoted from in His earthly ministry (Pss. 2; 22).

      d. The author of Hebrews quotes Psalm 22 in such a way that he implies that Jesus is the ultimate author of the Psalms (Heb. 2:12).

      e. Jesus is able to speak even the psalms of confession because He is our Mediator, confessing our sins before God as His own.

C. Tracing the connection of the Old Testament to the New Testament presents us with a difficulty that must be overcome in order to grow in our love for the Psalms.

  1. The Psalms contain the types and shadows of the old covenant but they are not overshadowed by the realities of the new covenant.

      a. The Psalms are an immediate word for partakers in the new covenant as already seen by how they are quoted in the book of Hebrews.

        b. The temptation is to think that the Psalms are irrelevant whenever they speak in Hebrew cultic language (e.g., sacrifices, Jerusalem, the temple).

        c. In reality, these images point us to their fulfillment in Jesus Christ, the new Jerusalem and the heavenly temple.

        d. As the types and shadows of the old covenant are fulfilled in Christ, we are able to fully enter into the heart of the Psalter in praise.

  2. The Psalms contain the history and struggle of God's people, which has direct relevance to our modern experience as God's people.

        a. Psalm 83 recounts the conspiracy of the nations to destroy Israel, and at first glance, this account may seem distant and irrelevant.

        b. Connecting the Old Testament with the New Testament helps us to see the relevance of such a psalm to the experience of the church.

D. Finding the themes of the Psalms presents us with a difficulty that must be overcome in order for us to grow in our love for the Psalms.

  1. God's goodness and unfailing love for the righteous is the great theme of the Psalms, a grand objective truth that evokes our subjective response of praise.

  2. God's goodness and unfailing love for the righteous is accompanied by three subordinate themes in the Psalms.

        a. The sinfulness of the righteous is prominently seen in psalms of confession and lamentation.

        b. The mystery of providence is prominently seen in psalms that question the suffering of the righteous and the success of the wicked.

        c. The confidence in God and the future is also seen weaved throughout the Psalms in prayers for relief and songs of praise.

STUDY QUESTIONS

  1. What is another way to translate the Hebrew word for "meditation"?

        a. "Focus"

        b. "Repeat"

        c. "Delight"

        d. "Mutter"

  2. How are the distinct images found in Psalm 23 held together?

        a. The first motif naturally progresses into the second motif.

        b. It is a great comfort that God is both our Shepherd and our King.

        c. The unifying principle of Hebrew poetry is found at a poem's center.

        d. Individual psalms need to be considered as one contextual unit.

  3. The Psalms are the third most quoted and alluded-to book of the Old Testament in the New Testament.

        a. True

        b. False

4. What is the clear implication of the author of Hebrew's quoting Psalm 22 in relation to Jesus?
   a. His throne is forever.
   b. He created the world.
   c. He spoke through David.
   d. He is greater than all the angels.

5. What was the primary argument against the idea that Jesus is speaking in the Psalms?
   a. David wrote a majority of the Psalms.
   b. The New Testament never makes such a claim.
   c. Jesus can't speak the psalms of confession of sin.
   d. The Psalms point to events before Jesus' earthly ministry began.

6. The connection between the Old and New Testament in the Psalms is relevant to the church in today's cultural climate because of which of the following?
   a. It teaches the church how the entire Bible is relevant.
   b. The opposition against the church is becoming more apparent. It helps us focus on the new covenant as the substance of the old.
   c. The fulfillment of Old Testament types will lead us to deeper praise.

DISCUSSION QUESTIONS

1. Take a moment to read a psalm slowly. How did reading a psalm this way change the way you experienced it? Was there anything surprising that you found in your reading?

2. Why is it important to understand all of the psalms as royal psalms? How does this understanding change the way you view the Psalms, especially as concerns the person and work of Christ?

3. Why do you think someone might be challenged in connecting the Old and New Testament in the Psalms? How would you help someone with such a difficulty see their connection? How would this change the way they read the Psalms?

4. How does the overarching theme and the underlying, subordinate themes of the Psalms lead us in prayer?

3
Psalm 11:
The Power of Poetry

INTRODUCTION

Psalm 11 exhibits the powerful characteristics of Hebrew poetry typically found throughout the Psalms. In this lesson, Dr. Godfrey uses Psalm 11 to provide us with an interpretive grid that we may apply to all the psalms as Hebrew poetry.

LESSON OBJECTIVES

1. To identify the characteristic traits of Hebrew poetry as found in Psalm 11
2. To highlight the structure of Psalm 11 to draw out the beauty of Scripture

SCRIPTURE READING

In the LORD I take refuge; how can you say to my soul, "Flee like a bird to your mountain, for behold, the wicked bend the bow; they have fitted their arrow to the string to shoot in the dark at the upright in heart."

—Psalm 11:1–2

LECTURE OUTLINE

A. Psalm 11 has a structure that is typical of other psalms, so by examining its structure we will know how to better read other psalms.

　1. Identifying the structure of a psalm will deepen our appreciation of a psalm.

　2. The first step in identifying the structure of a psalm is to read it in its entirety.

　3. Psalm 11 has a clear movement from distress to a confidence in the Lord as judge and vindicator of His people.

　　a. Psalm 11 begins with the dilemma of God's king as he faces the faithless advice to flee from the wicked.

　　b. Psalm 11 ends with the response of God's king to his advisers, which points us to the middle of the psalm to discover his rationale.

4. Psalm 11:4 is the heart of the psalm, orienting our thoughts so that we can make sense of what has come before and what comes after.

    a. The heart of Psalm 11 is "The LORD is in his holy temple; The LORD's throne is in heaven."

    b. David does not heed the counsel against his earthly throne because he is comforted by the reality that God is on His heavenly throne.

    c. The vivid imagery at the beginning and the end of Psalm 11 tempts us to overlook the heart of Psalm 11 that God remains on His throne.

5. Psalm 11 symmetrically revolves around the truth of God's sovereignty.

    a. The symmetry of Psalm 11 is found by looking at its first, middle, and last verses (Ps. 11:1, 4, 7).

    b. The symmetry of Psalm 11 presents an argument of calm confidence: David takes refuge in the God, knowing that the righteous will see His face, because He sits enthroned in heaven.

B. The meaning revealed in the symmetry of Psalm 11 anchors our understanding of David's response to his royal advisors.

1. Psalm 11 immediately moves away from the psalmist's contemplation of God as his refuge and security to the question, "How can you say to my soul?"

    a. David exhibits steadfast faithfulness and confidence in God by questioning the counsel of his royal advisers to flee.

    b. David's confidence is further expressed by the psalms' depiction of the wicked, who have only one arrow (Ps. 11:2).

2. Psalm 11 is not only an example of the faithfulness of God's king but is also an example of how the Psalms are unflinchingly truthful about our emotions.

    a. The question David presses upon his advisers resonates with us; we are often people who counsel ourselves with hopelessness.

    b. We often allow the visible realities of our lives to dominate the way we think, blinding ourselves from the reality that God is on His throne.

    c. Christians have difficulty expressing these types of frustrations, but the Psalms give voice to such fears and struggles in order to move us beyond them.

C. The heart of Psalm 11 helps us to look beyond the difficulties of our present reality and understand God's goodness, righteousness, and love.

1. The central word of the Psalm 11 teaches us that living by faith is believing in the truthfulness of what is unseen.

    a. One of the greatest struggles of faith is to think that God isn't paying attention to our struggles.

    b. Psalm 11 assures us that God is in control, wisely working out His good and sovereign plan according to the purposes of His will.

2. Psalm 11 points to the reality of a coming judgment of the wicked and thus teaches us about the righteousness of God.
   a. We tend to live in an age where the love of God is emphasized to such an extent that the reality of God's hatred is overlooked.
   b. It must be remembered that the cross is the place where God's love and God's hatred meet.
   c. If we do not see the judgment and the redemption of God at the cross, the cross loses any real significance.
   d. We must maintain the certainty of God's judgment upon the wicked.
3. Psalm 11 ends with the foundational truth of God's righteousness.
   a. Just as God hates the wicked for their wicked deeds, He loves the righteous for their righteous deeds.
   b. Despite the realities that prompted the faithless advice, David concludes in confidence that he will one day behold God's face.
4. The structure of Psalm 11 is a testimony to God's inspired Word, prompting us to meditate further on the Psalms and influencing the way we worship.

STUDY QUESTIONS

1. What is the first step you should take to familiarize yourself with a psalm?
   a. Determine the genre of the psalm
   b. Identify the center of the psalm
   c. Read the entire psalm
   d. Outline the psalm

2. What is the emotional heart of Psalm 11?
   a. "In the LORD I take refuge."
   b. "The LORD is in his holy temple."
   c. "The LORD tests the righteous."
   d. "For the LORD is righteous."

3. The symmetry of Psalm 11 can be seen in the comparison of the many resources of the wicked to the many resources of God.
   a. True
   b. False

4. Which of the following did Dr. Godfrey use as a historical reference from the Psalms to portray the frustrations of God's people?
   a. Israel's slavery in Egypt
   b. Israel's warfare with Assyria
   c. Israel's division into two kingdoms
   d. Israel's lament over the destruction of the temple

5. What is another way to translate "Let him rain coals on the wicked" from Psalm 11:6?
    a. "Let him rain fire on the wicked."
    b. "Let him rain traps on the wicked."
    c. "Let him rain death on the wicked."
    d. "Let him rain sulfur on the wicked."

6. People commonly argue against the idea that God hates the wicked because of

    _____ .

    a. God's righteous and holy character
    b. God's love for us in giving His only Son
    c. God's purpose for all things to bring Him glory
    d. God's just demands as Creator over His creation

DISCUSSION QUESTIONS

1. How could you use Dr. Godfrey's approach to interpreting Psalm 11 as a starting point to discover the structure and meaning of other psalms?

2. Where does Psalm 11 point us in order to face our frustrations, fears, and difficulties? How can you apply the realities expressed in Psalm 11 to your life, the church, or the world?

3. In what ways does Psalm 11 help you to think about righteousness and unrighteousness? What is the primary characteristic of the psalmist's righteousness?

4. We tend to live in an age that emphasizes God's love to the exclusion of God's hatred. How is upholding the truth of a sure and certain judgment against all unrighteousness related to the cross of Jesus Christ?

4

Psalms 26 & 39: Peculiar Psalms

INTRODUCTION

Certain psalms raise difficult questions that require us to apply a biblical hermeneutic so that we can make appropriate distinctions about them. In this lesson, Dr. Godfrey focuses his attention on Psalms 26 and 39 as examples of so called "problematic" psalms.

LESSON OBJECTIVES

1. To underline the difficulties found in Psalm 26 and Psalm 39
2. To demonstrate how these difficulties are not difficulties after all

SCRIPTURE READING

Vindicate me, O Lord, for I have walked in my integrity, and I have trusted in the Lord without wavering

—Psalm 26:1

Look away from me, that I may smile again, before I depart and am no more!

—Psalm 39:13

LECTURE OUTLINE

A. Psalm 26 can seem to challenge our understanding of righteousness and sin.

   1. Any difficulty we find in Scripture is only an apparent difficulty; we must allow Scripture to correct us, acknowledging its perfection and our imperfection.
   2. Psalm 26 poses a challenge to us because of an apparent contradiction with the Bible's representation of man as sinful and man as righteous.
      a. David describes himself as blameless in Psalm 26:1, yet he says "no living man is righteous" in Psalm 143:2.

15

      b.   The difficulty of Psalm 26:1 then becomes finding the appropriate relationship between it and other passages like Psalm 143:2.

   3.   Psalm 26 must be understood within the context of a distinction found running throughout the psalm: the distinction between the godly and the ungodly.

      a.   We know a considerable amount about David's life and about David's sin, so we know that David is not calling himself sinless in Psalm 26:1.

      b.   Paul uses the same language found in Psalm 26:1 to describe his labor to the churches as blameless—not sinless but faithful.

      c.   David is drawing a contrast between himself and the wicked; David is faithfully in covenant with God and, relative to the wicked, blameless.

      d.   On the other hand, David does not consider himself blameless relative to a holy God, which is how we should interpret Psalm 143:2.

   4.   The distinction between the godly and the ungodly found in the Psalms aims to teach us that our lives should be markedly different from those in the world.

   5.   The doctrine of sin must be balanced by the doctrines of justification and regeneration, allowing us to acknowledge our standing relative to the world.

      a.   Acknowledging that we are righteous relative to the world honors the work of Christ, the grace of God, and the gift of faith in justification.

      b.   Acknowledging that we are righteous relative to the world honors the renewing work of the Holy Spirit in regeneration.

   6.   The context of Psalm 26 clearly shows that David acknowledges his integrity before God as well as his need for redemption from God (Ps. 26:11).

   7.   David's prayer for redemption in Psalm 26:11 teaches us an important lesson about earnestly praying for the things God has promised to us.

      a.   A common misconception about the nature of promises is that we do not need to pray for what has already been promised.

      b.   Our relationship with God is a personal relationship; we do not relate to God as if He were a machine, so we converse with Him in prayer.

      c.   David does not pray doubting that God will redeem him, but rather he prays knowing that God is the only one who can redeem him.

B.   Psalm 39 is a difficult psalm because of the raw emotions to which it gives voice and the questions it raises concerning beliefs about the afterlife in the Old Testament.

   1.   Psalm 39 begins with the psalmist's reflection on a series of duties that lead him to complain, worry, and lament.

      a.   The psalmist has failed in the duty not to complain against the difficult providence brought about by the wicked.

      b.   His complaint and failure concerning his duties manifests itself in his worries about death and the discipline of the Lord.

      c.   The culmination of his weariness is expressed: "Look away from me, that I may smile again, before I depart and am no more!" (Ps. 39:13).

2. Psalm 39 is intriguing because of what the face of God represents and how unique the request of the psalmist is within the Psalter.
   a. The prayer of the psalmist throughout the Psalter is for God to turn His face toward him and not away from him as in Psalm 39.
   b. The face of God is synonymous with blessing; its significance can be seen in the Aaronic benediction (Num. 6:22–26).
3. Psalm 39 reminds us of the truthfulness of the Psalms in its expression of the full range of our emotions.
   a. Calvin believed that the emotions expressed in Psalm 39 are not appropriate for the "calm faith" of the Christian.
   b. Calvin also acknowledged that the emotions expressed in Psalm 39 prove that Christians can indeed feel overwhelmed at times.
4. Psalm 39 raises questions about the ancient beliefs in the afterlife: "Look away from me, that I may smile again, *before I depart and am no more.*"
   a. Refrains like "before I depart and am no more" have led some to question the existence of an Old Testament belief in an afterlife.
   b. Psalm 39 does not undermine the Old Testament belief in the afterlife, which is clearly taught elsewhere in Scripture (e.g., Ps. 23:6).
5. Psalm 39 must be interpreted within the scope of Israel's religious worship and corporate life.
   a. Israel expressed and fulfilled its worship and devotion to God in terms of the physical realities of Jerusalem and the temple.
   b. Psalm 39 stresses the importance of fulfillment in the worship of God, affirming this life but not denying the afterlife.

STUDY QUESTIONS

1. What is the apparent difficulty of Psalm 26 a product of?
   a. Our pharisaical attitude toward the world
   b. Our ability to identify with David
   c. Our awareness of David's sin
   d. Our translations of Scripture

2. What key theme found throughout the Psalms is highlighted in Psalm 26?
   a. The total depravity of man
   b. The promise of the coming Messiah
   c. The faithfulness of God to His people
   d. The distinction between the godly and the ungodly

3. David considers himself to be inherently righteous in Psalm 26.
   a. True
   b. False

4. Why makes the language of Psalm 39 unique in comparison to other psalms?
   a. The psalmist's depiction of death
   b. The psalmist's deep emotional lament
   c. The psalmist's use of technical Hebrew expressions
   d. The psalmist's request for God to turn away His face

5. What did Calvin believe about the emotions of Psalm 39?
   a. They could never be felt by Christians.
   b. They should normalize such feelings in the Christian life.
   c. They should be understood as uncharacteristic of Christian faith.
   d. They could be used to question the psalmist's belief in the afterlife.

6. The psalmist's remark about death and dying in Psalm 39 must be understood within the context of the _____ .
   a. Developing beliefs about the afterlife in the Old Testament
   b. Religious beliefs inherited by the Hebrews while in Egypt
   c. Centrality of corporate worship in the lives of Israelites
   d. Emotional distress of the psalmist leading to disbelief

DISCUSSION QUESTIONS

1. Reflecting on your life before Christ, how do you think your life is different now from what it would have been if you had never come to know Christ? Does reflecting on this help you make sense of the apparent difficulty of Psalm 26?

2. Why might Christians find it difficult to view themselves as righteous relative to the world? What dangers may arise from pride in our standing with God? How are these dangers avoided?

3. What do the apparent difficulties of Psalms 26 and 39 teach you about the proper interpretation of Scripture? What do these difficulties teach you about the proper attitude to bring to your study of Scripture?

4. Discuss the difficulty raised in Psalm 39 concerning Old Testament beliefs about the afterlife. How can Psalm 39 inform your understanding of Lord's Day worship?

5

Psalms 49 & 50: All the World & All the People

INTRODUCTION

Psalms 49 and 50 uniquely depart from the great theme of Book Two by focusing beyond the kingdom of God onto the world. In this lesson, Dr. Godfrey traces the progression of these psalms and explores what they tell us about the wisdom and worship of God.

LESSON OBJECTIVES

1. To contrast the wisdom of the world with the wisdom of God in Psalm 49
2. To communicate God's passion for heartfelt worship from Psalm 50

SCRIPTURE READING

But God will ransom my soul from the power of Sheol, for he will receive me.

—Psalm 49:15

The one who offers thanksgiving as his sacrifice glorifies me; to one who orders his way rightly I will show the salvation of God!

—Psalm 50:23

LECTURE OUTLINE

A. Every psalm in Book Two of the Psalter is centered on Jerusalem, the king, or the temple with the exception of Psalm 49; therefore, Psalm 49 warrants a closer look.

1. The emphasis on wisdom in Psalm 49 makes it sound like a proverb, and its emphasis on the world makes it a standout psalm in context of Book Two.

   a. Psalm 48 sets up Psalm 49 in its celebration of Jerusalem and the glories of Zion by noting them as the "joy of all the earth" (Ps. 48:1).

    b.   God's interest in Israel has never been separated from His concern for the whole world; Israel was the staging point for the gospel.

  2. Psalm 49 is a wisdom psalm that divides itself into two stanzas.

    a.   Stanza 1 (vv. 5–12) concerns the wisdom of the world; stanza 2 (vv. 12–20) concerns the wisdom of God.

    b.   Psalm 49 intends us to explore the ways and wisdom of the world before revealing how God takes us beyond the wisdom of the world.

B. Psalm 49 exposes worldly wisdom by its answer to the question, "Why should I fear in times of trouble?"

  1. The wisdom of the world answers the question posed in verses 5–6 with the grim reality of the inescapability of death.

    a.   The only comfort to those suffering at the hands of the rich in Psalm 49 is the fact that death is the great equalizer.

    b.   The world is strangely comforted by the inescapability of death, believing that all of our ends will be the same.

  2. Ironically, just as the downtrodden can see death as a comfort, the powerful simultaneously deny mortality, boasting in their resources (v. 13).

    a.   The wisdom of the world is capable of both ignoring the reality of death and finding comfort in it.

    b.   The contrary wisdom of the world progresses Psalm 49 to the wisdom of God and a reality greater than death—our redemption.

C. The wisdom of God in Psalm 49 can be briefly summarized: "The wicked are going to die and the righteous are going to live."

  1. The highlight of Psalm 49 is the reality that God will ransom His people, and they therefore have a hope for the future beyond death in the resurrection.

    a.   The wicked are being shepherded by death, never to see light again, but the ransomed "shall rule over them in the morning" (v. 14).

    b.   Morning is a significant theme in the Psalms that points to our confident hope and faith in God for our future (Ps. 30:5).

  2. The principle of ransom is important in the Old Testament because it is an essential lesson that God wants us to learn about His work of redemption, namely, that payment is required to atone for our sin.

  3. The principle of ransom can be clearly seen on display in the laws of the Old Testament and in Israel's redemption from Egypt.

    a.   God required Pharaoh to pay the death of his firstborn so that He could ransom His firstborn, Israel, from Egypt.

    b.   Just as God ransomed Israel, the psalmist is confident that God will be true to His redemptive character and ransom him from death.

4. Psalm 49 reveals that the difference between the wisdom of the world and the wisdom of God is understanding (vv. 12, 20).

D. Psalm 50 continues to expand upon the universal nature of Psalm 49 in order to center us on God's passion for right and true worship.

1. Psalm 50 is a judgment scene that begins with God's surprising summons of the whole earth to behold the judgment of His very own people.

2. God's summons of the whole the earth to bear witness against His people clearly indicates His passion for right and true worship.

   a. A statement that could be made to summarize the entire Old Testament: God is passionate about His worship.

   b. John Calvin believed the primary reason for the Reformation was the reformation of worship because worship is where we meet God.

3. God summons the whole earth to complain about two types of people relative to their attitudes in worship.

   a. Verses 7–15 focuses our attention on those who do not recognize that worship is a gift from God and not merely a rote requirement.

   b. Verses 16–23 focuses our attention on those who are numbered among the wicked, who make God in their own image.

4. The universal nature of Psalm 50 returns to the great themes of Book Two in the Psalter, reorienting and leading His people in repentance to consider His glory and worship accordingly.

STUDY QUESTIONS

1. Why is it surprising that Psalm 49 is situated in Book Two of the Psalter?
   a. Psalm 49 reintroduces the theme of Book One.
   b. Psalm 49 offers wisdom in a proverbial manner.
   c. Psalm 49 reveals God's purpose to bless the world.
   d. Psalm 49 shifts focus away from the glory of God's kingdom.

2. What reality is highlighted in Psalm 49 as a comfort of the righteous?
   a. Death
   b. Wisdom
   c. Ransom
   d. Judgment

3. The oppressed in Psalm 49 acknowledge the wisdom of the world in the same way their oppressors acknowledge the wisdom of the world.
   a. True
   b. False

4. What is the psalmist's intention in beginning Psalm 50 with three different names for God?
    a. To intensify God's name with a majestic plural
    b. To establish the cadence of the psalm
    c. To evoke the triune nature of God
    d. To arrest the reader's attention

5. What did Calvin believe was the primary concern of the Reformation?
    a. The reformation of worship
    b. The recovery of evangelical truth
    c. The right ordering of ecclesiastical authority
    d. The reorientation of God's people on the Word

6. According to Psalm 50, why does God condemn the wicked relative to right and proper worship?
    a. They worship God from a thankless heart.
    b. They worship God in a casual and mechanical fashion.
    c. They fail to recognize that worship is intended for their benefit.
    d. They fail to recognize that God is entirely different from themselves.

DISCUSSION QUESTIONS

1. What is the logic behind the wisdom of the world? How is the wisdom of God different and in what manner of life would someone who exercises it live?

2. What are different examples of restitution and ransom found throughout the Bible? Why is this such an important biblical concept in the economy of redemption?

3. In one sense Psalm 49 is an unusual psalm in Book Two, but in another sense its presence in Book Two shouldn't surprise us. How do Psalms 48, 49, and 50 naturally relate to one another?

4. Psalm 50 addresses two improper attitudes toward the worship of God. Why are these attitudes in worship offensive to God and how can you guard your heart against them?

6

Psalm 52:
The Psalms & History

INTRODUCTION

Psalm 52 refers to a specific historic event in the life of David and serves as an indictment against Doeg the Edomite. In this lesson, Dr. Godfrey explores the context of Psalm 52 to showcase the importance of history in interpretation.

LESSON OBJECTIVES

1. To narrate the tragic historical events that stand behind Psalm 52
2. To answer questions about the imprecatory psalms raised by Psalm 52

SCRIPTURE READING

Why do you boast of evil, O mighty man? The steadfast love of God endures all the day.

—Psalm 52:1

But I am like a green olive tree in the house of God. I trust in the steadfast love of God forever and ever.

—Psalm 52:8

LECTURE OUTLINE

A. The title of Psalm 52 references a specific historical event found in 1 Samuel 20–22.

   1. David was anointed king over Israel while Saul was still reigning as king, so Saul was embittered against him and was determined to kill him.

      a. In 1 Samuel 20–21, David flees Saul and comes to the tabernacle of God at Nob, where Ahimelech the priest gives him holy bread and the sword of Goliath.

      b. Doeg the Edomite, a herdsman attempting to win Saul's favor, reports David's location and Ahimelech's actions to Saul.

2. In 1 Samuel 22, the narrative records that Saul was in Gibeah when Doeg the Edomite supplied him with the necessary information to find David.
    a. Gibeah was a notorious town in the tribe of Benjamin involved in the rape and murder of a young woman (Judg. 19).
    b. The husband of the women divided her body into twelve pieces and sent them to the twelve tribes in order to demand justice, an act that led to civil war.
3. The narrative of 1 Samuel is foreshadowing Saul's ruthlessness by calling to mind the treacherous history of Gibeah.
    a. Saul sees Ahimelech's actions as treasonous and orders his soldiers to kill Ahimelech and all the other priests in the town of Nob.
    b. Saul's soldiers refuse to lift their swords against the Lord's anointed priest, but Doeg willingly kills Ahimelech and the other priests.
4. First Samuel 20–22 recounts a critical moment in the history of Israel as the right to the throne and the fate of the priesthood hang in the balance.
    a. First Samuel 20–22 and Psalm 52 remind us that none of the stories of the Bible are trivial.
    b. As Christians, we are connected to David's history and Israel's history, and David commemorated this portion of our history with a psalm.

B. Psalm 52 demonstrates the basic truth that the more history we know about a psalm the more the language of a psalm will be unveiled by its history.
1. The historical context of Psalm 52 reveals that David's reference to a "mighty man" in verse 1 is steeped with irony.
    a. Doeg the Edomite wasn't a mighty man; David stood in the company of mighty men who fought for him; Doeg was Saul's chief herdsman.
    b. Doeg the Edomite was a coward who killed 85 unarmed priests and the men, women, children, and livestock of Nob (1 Sam. 22:18–19).
2. David uses artful variation to contrast the fleeting evil of Doeg the Edomite with the steadfast love of the Lord, which "endures all the day" (Ps. 52:1).
3. Psalm 52 depicts the destructive power of the tongue through the tragic consequences of Doeg's lie about the priest's conspiracy against Saul.

C. Psalm 52 centers on the theme of God's judgment and justice and raises questions about the nature and place of the imprecatory psalms in the lives of Christians.
1. "But God will break you down forever" is the center of Psalm 52, and David is righteous to pray in anticipation that God will justly avenge Himself.
    a. Doeg was a vile man fully aware of his evil; even Saul's soldiers bear witness against him in their unwillingness to kill the priests.
    b. Doeg was not concerned with the law or the priesthood of God; he was only concerned with his material advancement through Saul.
2. Psalm 52 raises questions about the place of the imprecatory psalms—those psalms that call down God's judgment upon His enemies—in the Christian life.

  a. As Christians, we are not to pray for judgment against our enemies, for Christ has called us to love our enemies.

  b. However, the call to love our enemies does not mean it is wrong to pray for God to judge His enemies.

  c. Paul maps out the Christian life in Romans 12 and places emphasis on our peaceable lives with the fact that vengeance belongs to God.

  d. Paul teaches that love for our enemies is not an absolute ethical principle because it doesn't extend into eternity; God will repay.

 3. Imprecatory psalms must be understood in the greater context of the Psalms, in which the call to repentance comes before judgment (Pss. 9:10; 10:4–15).

  a. The imprecatory psalms are for those who refuse to repent.

  b. God would have been merciful to Doeg if he would have repented, but Doeg rejoiced in his evil and refused refuge in God (Ps. 52:7).

D. David responded to Doeg the Edomite's wickedness and the reality of God's coming final judgment by reflecting on God's preserving hand in his life.

 1. David understood that God had preserved him: "But I am like a green olive tree in the house of God" (Ps. 52:8).

 2. God's steadfast love extends to the priests of Nob, who though slaughtered by Doeg the Edomite will dwell in the house of God forever.

 3. Psalm 52 contrasts those who will be destroyed by the Lord with those who will dwell with Him in His house forever.

STUDY QUESTIONS

 1. Why does Doeg the Edomite report David's whereabouts to Saul?

  a. He is a victim desiring revenge against David.

  b. He is a soldier following the orders of the king.

  c. He is a herdsman seeking the favor of the king.

  d. He is a priest defending the honor of the tabernacle.

 2. Why was Saul's location in Gibeah mentioned in 1 Samuel 22?

  a. To foreshadow Saul's ruthlessness

  b. To foreshadow Saul's future dethronement

  c. To indicate Saul's awareness of David's location

  d. To indicate Saul's power within the tribe of Benjamin

 3. Knowing the history behind Psalm 52 is important to catch David's irony in referring to Doeg the Edomite as a "mighty man."

  a. True

  b. False

4. Which of the following themes is at the center of Psalm 52?
   a. Saul's villainy
   b. Doeg's violence
   c. David's vexation
   d. God's vengeance

5. What is the emphasis in Psalm 52 on the destructiveness of a deceitful tongue in reference to?
   a. Doeg's lie to David about his allegiance
   b. Doeg's lie to Ahimelech to gather information
   c. Doeg's lie to Saul about David's wicked intentions
   d. Doeg's lie to Saul about the priests' conspiracy against him

6. Whom should the imprecatory psalms be prayed against?
   a. Those who commit heinous sin
   b. Those who refuse to repent before God
   c. Those who fall beyond God's saving love
   d. Those who declare themselves your enemy

DISCUSSION QUESTIONS

1. Why is the history of Psalm 52 important to the history of Israel? Why is the history of Psalm 52 important to Christians?

2. What are some factors that indicate the extent of Doeg the Edomite's sin and justify David's prayer of indictment against him? What are some key characteristics about David that stand in contrast to Doeg in Psalm 52?

3. Is it right for Christians to pray the imprecatory psalms? Why or why not? What important distinctions must be made to understand the place of the imprecatory psalms in the Christian life?

4. Why are imprecatory psalms particularly difficult to understand in our day? What truths about the character of God and the free offer of the gospel should balance someone's perspective of the imprecatory psalms?

7

Psalm 77: Questions in Grief

INTRODUCTION

Psalm 77 is characteristic of the psalms of crisis in Book Three of the Psalter, but unlike many of these psalms, it ends in hope. In this lesson, Dr. Godfrey employs Psalm 77 as the key to an appropriate response to God in our times of trouble.

LESSON OBJECTIVES

1. To convey the deep emotional distress of the psalmist in Psalm 77
2. To promote appropriate attitudes toward God in prayer and meditation

SCRIPTURE READING

In the day of my trouble I seek the Lord; in the night my hand is stretched out without wearying; my soul refuses to be comforted.

—Psalm 77:2

I will remember the deeds of the LORD; yes, I will remember your wonders of old. I will ponder all your work, and meditate on your mighty deeds.

—Psalm 77:11–12

LECTURE OUTLINE

A. Filled with psalms of crisis over God's promises, Book Three of the Psalms marks a drastic turn from the early themes in the Psalter, but Psalm 77 is a highlight of hope.

1. Book Three includes Psalms 73 through 89, psalms filled with lament, a sense of abandonment, and questions about God's faithfulness.
2. Psalm 77 is a psalm of deep distress characteristic of Book Three, but it also has a strong emphasis on comfort and encouragement in the midst of trouble.

3. Psalm 77:2 refers to "a day of trouble," a phrase that occurs a number of times throughout the Psalms.
   a. Sometimes "a day of trouble" refers to a particular event when used in the Psalms, but other times it refers to trouble generally.
   b. "A day of trouble" in Psalm 77 may allude to Jacob's response to the report of Joseph's death, so it may concern the death of a loved one.
4. Psalm 77 contains that same emotional honesty found throughout the Psalms with its themes of meditation, sleeplessness, and honest questioning.
   a. The psalmist of Psalm 77 is immensely distressed, sleeplessly meditating and crying out to God (vv. 2–4).
   b. Verse 5 foreshadows the hope of the psalmist as he looks to the faithfulness of the Lord before asking a series of haunting questions.

B. The questions of Psalm 77 reveal the psalmist's sense of abandonment, wrestling with whether God will be faithful to His promises.
   1. The 170 questions found throughout the Psalter demonstrate the liberating character of the Psalms that we do not have to pretend about our emotions.
   2. We can be honest with our feelings before God, because God never objects to His people coming to Him honestly in faith.
   3. Israel at Rephidim is used throughout Scripture as an example of how God's people can fail to approach Him in emotionally honest prayer (Ex. 17).
      a. Israel sinned in complaint to Moses after being brought out of Egypt, but emotionally honest prayer does not cause us to sin like Israel.
      b. The great offense of Israel was not that they brought their complaints before God; it was that Israel faithlessly grumbled as if behind God's back.
      c. We must feel the freedom to come before God honestly in faith, not in faithless grumbling, but in true, heartfelt honesty that rightfully glorifies God.
   4. Psalm 77 is filled with rhetorical questions that inherently imply negative answers such as, "Has his steadfast love forever ceased?" (v. 8).
      a. Steadfast love is translated from the Hebrew word *chesed*, which the King James Version translates as "mercy."
      b. *Chesed* denotes God's covenant faithfulness, His love and mercy to His people in light of the covenant He promised would never fail.
   5. Rhetorical questions aside, Psalm 77 presents the honest questions of the psalmist in the dark moments of doubt and disillusion over God's promises.
      a. Psalms 77 discloses the disoriented heart of the psalmist, disoriented because of the intrinsically reliable nature of God's promises.
      b. Precisely because God's promises are always reliable, the psalmist assumes that God must be angry with him for an unbeknownst sin.

C. Psalm 77 teaches us what we are to do in our days of trouble: Remember the Lord.

   1. Verses 10–11 form the center of the psalm and focus our attention on what God's people should do in times of distress.

      a. Not only are we to pray honestly before God, but we are also to think about God's care and love for us as He has demonstrated in the past.

      b. By recalling God's mighty deeds in the past, we can be assured that He will not abandon us in the present or in the future.

   2. The psalmist models godly remembrance for us by recalling God's mighty work of redemption in the exodus of Israel from Egypt.

      a. The exodus is God's emblematic work of redemption in which He remembered Israel, led her across the sea, and defeated Pharaoh.

      b. Psalm 77 faithfully asks with Israel, after God mocked the gods of Egypt, "What god is great like our God?" (v. 13).

   3. Psalm 77 maintains a consistent strain as the psalmist meditates upon God's mighty work of redemption in light of Israel's uncertainty before the Red Sea.

      a. Amid lightning and thunder, Israel faced Pharaoh's army behind and the impassible sea ahead.

      b. Nonetheless, God led Israel through the sea even though His footprints were unseen (v. 19).

   4. Psalm 77 closes beautifully: "You led your people like a flock by the hand of Moses and Aaron" (v. 20).

      a. The closing verse of Psalm 77 draws attention to the repetition of the word "hand" throughout the psalm (vv. 2, 10, 20).

      b. As we raise our hands in prayer to Him, remembering the deeds of His hand, He is truly with us, even through those ministering to us.

STUDY QUESTIONS

   1. What may the "day of trouble" in Psalm 77 be an allusion to?
      a. Israel's lament over the destruction of the temple
      b. Jacob's response to the report of Joseph's death
      c. David's distress over Saul and Jonathan's death
      d. Israel's crisis of faith concerning God's promises

   2. Why makes Psalm 77 stand out in Book Three of the Psalter?
      a. Its strong emphasis on the faithfulness of God to His promises
      b. Its strong emphasis on the night spent in meditation and prayer
      c. Its strong emphasis on the emotional honesty required in prayer
      d. Its strong emphasis on the sleeplessness of a burdened conscience

   3. The questions found within Psalm 77 are all rhetorical questions in which the answer is implied in the question itself.
      a. True
      b. False

4. How many questions are asked throughout the Psalms to help confirm our feelings of uncertainty as valid feelings?
   a. 50
   b. 120
   c. 170
   d. 250

5. What is referenced throughout Scripture as emblematic of how we are not to respond to God in our trials and difficulties?
   a. Pharaoh's hardheartedness
   b. Saul's halfhearted obedience
   c. Israel's experience at Rephidim
   d. Israel's fear before the Red Sea

6. What does the keyword repetition found in Psalm 77 indicate?
   a. God's willingness to openly receive our prayers
   b. God's willingness to continually lead us by His hand
   c. God's willingness to always answer our difficult questions
   d. God's willingness to forever reveal Himself in acts of redemption

DISCUSSION QUESTIONS

1. What are the primary concerns of God's people in Book Three? How does Psalm 77 balance these concerns so that we may rightly respond before God?

2. How does God inform our prayer life through Israel's experience in the exodus and in the wilderness at Rephidim?

3. What are times when God has been faithful to you in the past that you could bring to mind when meditating and praying through hardship?

4. Our culture tends to stress individuality to the extent that seeing beyond ourselves can be difficult. How does the psalmist protect us against this mentality in Psalm 77? How do you plan to incorporate God's mighty works of corporate redemption into your prayer life?

Psalm 81:
The Word at the Center

INTRODUCTION

Psalm 81 can be said to be the most important psalm because of its placement at the center of the Psalter. In this lesson, Dr. Godfrey reviews the themes of Psalm 81, pointing out how they ultimately center on the Lord Jesus Christ.

LESSON OBJECTIVES

1. To explain Psalm 81 as the organizing principle at the center of the Psalter
2. To examine Psalm 81 in light of Jesus' fulfillment of the Old Testament

SCRIPTURE READING

O Israel, if you would but listen to me!

—Psalm 81:8b

But my people did not listen to my voice.

—Psalm 81:11a

LECTURE OUTLINE

A. Psalm 81 is the central point in the Psalter, which makes it the most important psalm for making sense of the overarching theme of Israel's crisis in the Psalms.

1. Psalm 81 stands at the center of the Psalter, even though there are 150 psalms, because it is the central psalm in Book Three.

   a. Psalm 81 is arguably the most important psalm in the Psalter when considering the emphasis Hebrew poetry places on the center.

   b. Psalm 81, as an explanation of the history of Israel and the history of redemption, makes it an organizing principle of the whole of Scripture.

2. Psalm 81 focuses on one of the central texts in the Old Testament and the central holy day of Israel's liturgical calendar.

   a. Psalm 81:8 is the central point of the psalm, which echoes the *Shema* of Deuteronomy 6:4 and points to the primary problem of all mankind.

   b. Psalm 81:3 calls Israel to worship on the Feast of Tabernacles in the seventh month of Israel's liturgical calendar.

3. The language in Psalm 81:3 of the new moon and the full moon are meant to center the astute reader's attention on the Day of Atonement.

   a. The new moon marked the New Year in the seventh month of Israel's liturgical calendar; the full moon marked the Feast of Tabernacles.

   b. The Day of Atonement is the fast day situated between the new moon and the full moon of the seventh month.

   c. The Day of Atonement is the heart of Israel's year of worship, so in the central psalm we are brought to the center of Israel's worship.

B. Psalm 81 contains a word of deliverance, direction, and destruction to Israel.

   1. Psalm 81 calls Israel to listen to God's word of deliverance during this season of remembrance of God's renewing, forgiving, and provisional power.

   2. Psalm 81 uses the poetic device of allusion to develop upon God's mighty acts of deliverance.

      a. Psalm 81 readies us to meditate on the hardship of Israel's slavery: "I relieved your shoulder of the burden" (v. 6).

      b. Only after such vivid imagery and allusion to Israel's slavery does the psalmist speak directly of Israel's redemption from slavery in Egypt.

   3. God's word of deliverance in Psalm 81 is not only a word about His past acts of redemption but also a word of promise about His future acts of redemption.

   4. Psalm 81 calls Israel to listen to God's word as a directive for deliverance out of the crisis in which she finds herself because of her failures in right worship.

   5. The key way that God measures the faithfulness of His people concerns whether they will worship Him the way He has commanded them.

      a. Worship is a measure of obedience because if God's people are not obedient when they come before Him, they will not be obedient elsewhere.

      b. Verse 3 sets up the directive of Psalm 81 for Israel's remedy to disobedient worship: "O Israel, if you would but listen to me!"

   6. Israel's history demonstrates an unwillingness to abide by the most explicit commands of God concerning His worship.

      a. One of the most explicit commands God gives concerning His worship is His command against graven images (Ex. 20:4).

      b. Israel continually broke this commandment and chose instead to be as other nations, worshiping worthless idols made with human hands.

      c. We must not consider ourselves wiser than God, thinking we can improve upon His worship beyond what He has commanded.

   7. Psalm 81 calls Israel to listen to God's word to be delivered from patterns of false worship and the destruction of God's enemies.

C. Psalm 81 points to the Lord Jesus Christ, who listened to the Father perfectly, as our hope and redemption, that we may worship God from a true heart.

  1. Jesus is at the heart of Psalm 81; He has perfectly listened to the Father.
      a. The context of Psalm 81 is the prayer for deliverance in Psalm 80 in which is acknowledged the need of God's restoration by a Redeemer.
      b. Jesus is that Redeemer who understood the Word of deliverance, followed the Word of direction, and embraced the Word of destruction.

  2. Jesus succeeded in every way Israel failed.
      a. Psalm 81 reflects on three of Israel's problems in the wilderness: food, power, and worship.
      b. The wilderness temptations of Jesus demonstrate how He withstood against Satan over food, power, and worship (Matt. 4:1–11).

  3. The preparations of God in the history of Israel through institutions and signs come together in the person and work of Christ as the true Israel.
      a. Jesus is the fulfillment of the New Year, the Feast of Tabernacles, and the Day of Atonement.
      b. Psalm 81 helps us to understand the perfect obedience of Christ and helps us to worship God fully illumined by His gracious forgiveness.

STUDY QUESTIONS

  1. What does the center of Psalm 81 echo?
      a. The second commandment of Deuteronomy 5:8
      b. The Aaronic benediction of Numbers 6:24–26
      c. The Abrahamic covenant of Genesis 15
      d. The *Shema* of Deuteronomy 6:4

  2. What is the significance of the imperative, "Blow the trumpet at the new moon, at the full moon, on our feast day," in the third verse of Psalm 81?
      a. It shows how trumpets announced holy days of worship.
      b. It highlights the center of Israel's liturgical calendar.
      c. It alludes to the trumpet blasts of Mount Sinai.
      d. It commends Israel's pure worship.

  3. The argument that Psalm 81 is the center of the Psalter fails to recognize the simple fact that there are 150 psalms.
      a. True
      b. False

  4. What is the touchstone by which God measures our faithfulness?
      a. Teaching future generations about Him
      b. Willingness to give to His kingdom
      c. Displays of sacrificial love
      d. Obedience in worship

5. Which historic creedal document advances the idea that we are not to be "wiser than God" as related to how we are to worship Him?
    a. The Belgic Confession
    b. The Canons of Dort
    c. The Heidelberg Catechism
    d. The Westminster Confession of Faith

6. What is one of the most explicit commands God gives us about worship?
    a. We are to worship Him in song and dance.
    b. We are to worship Him without making images of Him.
    c. We are to worship Him with sensitivity to cultural norms.
    d. We are to worship Him morning and evening on the Lord's Day.

DISCUSSION QUESTIONS

1. Dr. Godfrey placed a considerable emphasis on Psalm 81 as the center of the Psalms. How does Psalm 81 as the center of the Psalter contribute to your understanding of the Psalms as a whole?

2. What is God's word of deliverance, direction, and destruction in Psalm 81? How do they make Psalm 81 just as relevant to the church today?

3. Dr. Godfrey argued that Psalm 81 is perhaps the most important psalm in the Psalter. What does that tell you about worship, and how does worship relate to the whole of the Christian life?

4. Contrasting the faithlessness of Israel with the faithfulness of Christ, how is Jesus the center of Psalm 81?

Psalms 91 & 93: God Is Protector & King

INTRODUCTION

From the beginning, God has revealed Himself as trustworthy, the great comfort that drives Book Four of the Psalms. In this lesson, Dr. Godfrey studies Psalms 91 and 93, two psalms of comfort that teach us where to go in times of crisis.

LESSON OBJECTIVES

1. To survey the overall theme of Book Four through various psalms
2. To study the amazing promises of angelic protection in Psalm 91
3. To highlight the poetic structure and emphasis of Psalm 93

SCRIPTURE READING

For he will command his angels concerning you to guard you in all your ways. On their hand they will bear you up, lest you strike your foot against a stone. You will tread on the lion and the adder; the young lion and the serpent you will trample underfoot.

—Psalm 91:11–13

Mightier than the thunders of many waters, mightier than the waves of the sea, the LORD on high is mighty!

—Psalm 93:4

LECTURE OUTLINE

A. Book Four of the Psalter is characterized by psalms that reflect on God's faithfulness in creation and covenant for encouragement.

1. Book Four teaches us how to move away from crises of faith by remembering God's faithfulness, particularly in creation and in covenant with Moses.

2. Psalm 90 is the first psalm of Book Four and is titled "A Prayer of Moses."
   a. The title of Psalm 90 immediately points God's people beyond the questions about the Davidic throne to the time of Moses.
   b. The first verses of Psalm 90 point further back to the theme of God's power in creation as a reason to look back to Him in hope.
3. Psalm 92 continues the theme of creation and is titled "A Song for the Sabbath," as the Sabbath was instituted at creation for our benefit.
4. Psalms 105 and 106 reflect on Israel's history, focusing on the blessings of God through the patriarchs and the affliction brought about by Israel's sin.
5. Book Four of the Psalter, even with its notes of comfort, still identifies a lingering crisis among God's people that will be resolved in Book Five.

B. Psalm 91 is a great meditation on the promises of God as they extended to Israel in exile; it affirms that days of loss would be followed by days of celebration and blessing.
   1. Psalm 91 meditates on the promises of God in Deuteronomy 32 and 33.
      a. Deuteronomy 31 explicitly states that God will come in judgment against His own people if they are unfaithful.
      b. Deuteronomy 31 and 32 extend the promises of God such that, even after judgment, He will return to them to bless and restore them.
   2. The introductory theme of Psalm 91 is the nearness of God, and because He is near to us, we have no reason to fear (vv. 4, 5).
      a. Psalm 91 uses vivid imagery to depict how God relates to us and protects us, comparing God to a bird sheltering us with His wings.
      b. Psalm 91 is not a promise that Christians will never know harm but a promise that God will be faithful to His people and protect them.

C. Psalm 91 proclaims the realities of God as our refuge, a theme highlighted by clear references to God's appointment of angels to protect and help us (vv. 11–13).
   1. Satan quoted from Psalm 91:11–12 when tempting Jesus in the wilderness.
      a. Satan attempted to use the Word of God against Jesus Christ, but Jesus wisely replied to the Devil's ruse, "It is written . . ." (Matt. 4:7).
      b. Jesus' answer to Satan is a demonstration of the hermeneutical principle that Scripture interprets Scripture.
   2. God created angels out of His love for diversity and purpose in His creation.
      a. God is all-powerful, so by definition, He doesn't need angels to carry out His will; nevertheless, God created angels out of His creative joy.
      b. God created angels also to carry out His divine purposes, that they would be ministering spirits for God's elect (Heb. 1:14).
   3. Popular notions about personal guardian angels are not supported biblically and are frivolous in comparison to God's promise to protect us.
   4. Satan tempted Jesus with a superficial and frivolous understanding of angels in the wilderness, but Jesus understood the real meaning of Psalm 91.

      a. The most frequent references to angels in the life of Jesus Christ occur in gospel of Matthew (1:20; 4:11; 25:31; 26:53; 28:2).

      b. Jesus, the Son of God, possessed rightful command over His angels, but He did not call upon them to deliver Him.

      c. Angels were found at every stage of Jesus' life, demonstrating that they helped Him do the Father's will as He trusted in the Father's protection.

   5. Notice that Satan did not quote Psalm 91:13: "You will tread on the lion and the adder; the young lion and the serpent you will trample underfoot."

D. Psalm 93 utilizes a rhythmic Hebrew poetic device to stress the theme of Book Four.

   1. Psalm 93 uses the rhythm of Hebrew syllables to direct the reader's speed and thus places the greatest emphasis on the longest verse, verse 5.

   2. Psalm 93 begins with a rapid-fire confession of God's majesty and slows to focus on the chaotic nature of the sea to juxtapose God's almighty power.

   3. Psalm 93 extols God's trustworthy statutes, directing us in confidence to His sovereign creating rule by His sustaining covenantal Word.

STUDY QUESTIONS

1. What characterizes the psalms of Book Four of the Psalter?
   a. A reflection on God's work in covenant and creation
   b. A reflection on God's promises in desperation and doubt
   c. A reflection on God's commitment to His people as individuals
   d. A reflection on God's commitment to His people as a community

2. Jesus responded to the devil's use of Psalm 91 by saying, "It is also written," which undergirds what principle of biblical hermeneutics?
   a. Scripture is to be interpreted with respect to literary genre.
   b. Scripture is to be interpreted by Scripture.
   c. Scripture is to be interpreted as the inspired Word of God.
   d. Scripture is to be interpreted within an immediate context.

3. Hebrew poetry, like Old English poetry, is based on rhyme.
   a. True
   b. False

4. Why did God create angels?
   a. To shelter Christians as personal guardians
   b. To help Christians understand God's will
   c. To keep Christians from physical harm
   d. To serve Christians as ministering spirits

5. In which gospel account do angels most frequently appear throughout the different stages of Jesus' life and ministry?
    a. Matthew
    b. Mark
    c. Luke
    d. John

6. What is emphasized at the slowest point of Psalm 93?
    a. The majesty and strength of God
    b. The uncontrollable nature of the sea
    c. The firm establishment of the cosmos
    d. The trustworthiness of God's statutes

DISCUSSION QUESTIONS

1. The theme of Psalm 91 is "God is near." What then are the implications of Psalm 91 for the Christian life?

2. How does a biblical understanding of angels differ from popular notions of angels in our surrounding culture?

3. How did Satan try to use God's Word against Jesus? Are you able to draw any comparisons between the temptations of Christ in the wilderness and the temptation of our first parents in the garden? Why didn't the devil quote all of Psalm 91?

4. Psalm 93 utilizes the symbolic nature of the sea as chaotic, powerful, and uncontrollable. How does this relate to the overall theme of Book Four of the Psalter?

Psalm 94:
Comfort from the Future

INTRODUCTION

God disciplines those He loves, and as His people, God's discipline should be a joy and a comfort. In this lesson, Dr. Godfrey draws our attention to the blessed man of Psalm 94 rejoicing in God's discipline while praying for judgment against the wicked.

LESSON OBJECTIVES

1. To promote a balanced and biblical understanding of God's just judgment
2. To discover the joy of God's discipline and the comfort of God's promises

SCRIPTURE READING

Blessed is the man whom you discipline, O Lord, and whom you teach out of you law.

—Psalm 94:12

For the Lord will not forsake his people; he will not abandon his heritage; for justice will return to the righteous, and all the upright in heart will follow it.

—Psalm 94:14–15

LECTURE OUTLINE

A. Psalm 94 breaks from the pattern of Book Four by looking at the promises of God in order to derive comfort for the future.

   1. The center of Psalm 94 is verse 12: "Blessed is the man whom you discipline. O Lord, and whom you teach out of your law." This is an echo of Psalm 1.

   2. Psalm 94:12 uses the Hebrew word for "blessed" from Psalm 1:1 but a different word for "man" with a slightly nuanced meaning.

a. The Hebrew for "man" in Psalm 94 and Psalm 1 both refer exclusively to males, but Psalm 94 uses a word that refers to young males.

b. The Hebrew for "blessed" in Psalm 94 and Psalm 1 is stative, referring to blessedness as a state of being, not an action.

c. The Hebrew may suggest the appropriateness of young men's looking forward in hope and certainly suggests that blessedness is an emotional state of happiness and well-being.

B. Psalm 94 is a prayer of judgment, even referencing God as the God of vengeance.

1. Psalm 94 is a prayer for God to answer the godly and bring to an end the distress caused by the triumph of the wicked because of their sin.

a. The Psalms teach that the crisis of the godly is sometimes a result of God's disciplining hand in reaction to the sinfulness of His people.

b. God would call on nations to carry Israel into exile as punishment for Israel's sin and yet promise to judge these nations for their actions.

c. The context of Psalm 94 is Israel's cry for judgment, looking forward to the certain and coming judgment of God against its oppressors.

2. The truth of God's judgment is often unpronounced in modern evangelicalism.

a. Christianity that only highlights God's love, mercy, and kindness apart from God's righteousness can be called "judgmentless Christianity," which is really no Christianity at all.

b. Biblical Christianity must maintain biblical tensions in order to preserve the scriptural truth that we serve a God of judgment *and* mercy.

3. The distress of the blessed man is Psalm 94 reflects a proper understanding of judgment through his desire to see the righteousness of God manifested.

a. Christianity balances a love for the wicked with a love for the future manifestation of God's righteousness in judgment over the wicked.

b. Christians can simultaneously pray for the conversion of the wicked and long for the day of salvation and God's coming judgment.

C. Psalm 94 reflects on the importance of understanding and the joy of God's discipline.

1. Psalm 94 calls for the ignorant, unthinking, and brutish to recognize the righteous ways of God and the judgment His righteousness demands.

a. The blessedness of the man in Psalm 94 isn't without understanding.

b. The blessedness of the man in Psalm 94 is a result of knowing the tragedy that befalls those who exist in rebellion apart from God.

2. Psalm 94 allows a voice of outrage to be lifted against the ways of the wicked precisely because the godly have an understanding that is not of this world.

a. Christians are able to have a genuine outrage over the tragic events of this world, whereas the world has no standard of righteousness.

b. Christians should only have a sense of outrage on behalf of God in proper recognition of His law and holiness.

  c. Outrage over the world's sinfulness in relation to God's righteousness should always be characterized by compassion and love.

 3. Psalm 94 teaches us that the wise never envy the lawless and clueless ways of the wicked but rather embrace the discipline of the Lord.

  a. Psalm 94 recognizes the folly of the wicked by cataloging their lawless deeds and raising rhetorical questions that extol God's knowledge.

  b. Psalm 94 likely reference God's discipline of Israel through exile, but even such harsh discipline is embraced by the humble.

D. Psalm 94 focuses on the fatherly promises of God alongside its call for judgment.

 1. Psalm 94 proves that those who God disciplines will not be abandoned, for God will not abandon His heritage; indeed, God is our helper (vv. 14, 17).

 2. Psalm 94 is filled with remarkable comforts, so in the midst of our crisis we can look to Him to cheer our souls; indeed, God is our stronghold (vv. 19, 22).

STUDY QUESTIONS

1. How does Psalm 94 break with the pattern of Book Four of the Psalter?
  a. By looking to the past to God's faithfulness in His creation
  b. By looking to the past to God's faithfulness in His covenant
  c. By looking to the present to God's faithfulness to His covenant
  d. By looking to the future to God's faithfulness to His righteousness

2. What the title given to God is exclusive to Psalm 94?
  a. God of wrath
  b. God of judgment
  c. God of vengeance
  d. God of anger

3. Calvin's use of Psalm 124 ("Our help is in the name of the Lord, the maker of heaven and earth") to begin each worship gathering in Geneva is unique in the history of the church.
  a. True
  b. False

4. What must be allowed to stand beside a love for the lost in sound, biblical theology?
  a. A desire for the sudden conversion of the wicked
  b. A desire for the swift condemnation of the wicked
  c. A desire for the success of gospel ministry worldwide
  d. A desire for the righteousness of God to be manifested

5. In light of the crisis of faith characteristic of Book Three, what is the discipline of the Lord in Psalm 94 most likely a reference to?
   a. The unwarranted attacks against Israel from the nations
   b. The sinfulness of David as representative of Israel
   c. The failure of Israel to be a light unto the nations
   d. The harsh exile of Israel resulting from sin

6. What does Calvin say is the beginning of religion?
   a. Humility
   b. Understanding
   c. Teachableness
   d. Reverence

DISCUSSION QUESTIONS

1. How does Psalm 94 give voice to an appropriate outrage over world events? What should always govern our sense of outrage as Christians?

2. What does the life of a Christian who understands the great value of God's discipline look like? How is his or her walk characterized in times of abundance and plenty and in times of trial and tribulation?

3. How do understanding, wisdom, and humility contribute to the blessed state of the man of Psalm 94? How is he contrasted with the wicked?

4. Dr. Godfrey described the modern aversion to judgment and its influence on evangelicalism as "judgmentless Christianity." Describe "judgmentless Christianity." How does it portray God? How does it portray the person and work of Christ?

Psalm 127:
The Lord's Beloved

INTRODUCTION

Psalm 127 sits at the center of the Psalms of Ascents, and the center of Psalm 127 points to Christ, our King. In this lesson, Dr. Godfrey expounds Psalm 127, pointing the way to Jesus—the fulfillment of Israel—as reflected in King Solomon.

LESSON OBJECTIVES

1. To explain the internal structure of Book Five of the Psalter
2. To reveal the Christ-centeredness of Psalm 127

SCRIPTURE READING

He gives to his beloved sleep.

—Psalm 127:2b

Behold, a voice from heaven said, "This is my beloved Son, with whom I am well pleased.

—Matthew 3:17

LECTURE OUTLINE

A. Book Five of the Psalter exhibits a beautifully intentional structure and organization as it chronologically progresses through Israel's history.

1. Psalm 107 begins Book Five with God's promise to restore His people.
2. Psalm 110 looks forward in messianic expectation and is situated within a series of psalms concerning struggles and glories of the king of Israel.
3. Psalm 113 through 118 reflect on God's great work of deliverance, psalms Jews sing in celebration of the Passover called "The Egyptian Hallel."
4. Psalm 119 celebrates God's law, and immediately after psalms about the exodus, it is chronologically situated in Israel's history.

5. Psalm 120 through 134 comprise the Psalms of Ascents, psalms rejoicing in Israel's annual pilgrimages to Jerusalem.

6. Psalm 135 through 137 return to the struggle of Israel, following the history of Israel chronologically in Book Five from Egypt to Sinai to Jerusalem to exile.

7. Psalms 138 through 145, as Davidic psalms, focus on the restoration of the king and the kingdom, helping to resolve the crisis of Book Three.

B. The Psalms of Ascents center on Israel's pilgrimages to Jerusalem as formative to Israel's collective identity, chiefly in Psalm 127, which further centers on Israel's king.

1. Psalm 127 resides at the center of the Psalms of Ascents. The psalm itself centers on its author, Solomon, and its ultimate author, Jesus Christ.
    a. Solomon's reign expressed the greatest glory of the Davidic kingship.
    b. The splendor and glory of Solomon's earthly kingdom represents the splendor and glory of Jesus Christ, who rules and reigns perfectly.

2. Psalm 127 recognizes and celebrates the truth that all our successes come from God—without Him, all of our labors are in vain (vv. 1–2).
    a. Psalm 127:1a is intentionally ambiguous as "home" could be referring to an ordinary home, the king's palace, or God's temple.
    b. Psalm 127:1b is reminiscent of Psalm 48 as a celebration of the walls of Jerusalem with a special emphasis on God as its sure defender.
    c. Psalm 127:2 is a clear reference to God as a provider, acknowledging the anxiety of work in an agricultural society reliant on the weather.
    d. Psalm 127:2b, "For he gives to his beloved rest," is at the center of the psalm, pointing to the refreshment and renewal of sleep.

3. Psalm 127 continues the theme of dependence on the Lord by developing the image of life as a community absolutely dependent on one another.
    a. Children were absolutely necessary to help with the work of the farm, to provide for their parents in old age, and to defend the nation.
    b. Children should not be sentimentalized using the Psalms; children were essential for Israel's survival and a blessing from the Lord.

C. Psalm 127 centers on Solomon's artful self-reference, which emphasizes the importance of the king as representative of Israel and the faithfulness of Christ.

1. The central verse of Psalm 127, "For He gives his beloved sleep," references the name given to Solomon by David and the name given to him by the Lord.
    a. David named his son Solomon, which is derived from the Hebrew word *shalom*, and evokes the notion of peaceful sleep.
    b. God renamed Solomon in 2 Samuel 12:25 to Jedidiah, which means "beloved of the Lord," making Psalm 127:2 an allusion to both names.

2. Solomon's placement at the center of Psalm 127 indicates God's desire for His people to reflect on the importance of the king as a representative.
    a. The king of Israel was to represent what God would ultimately accomplish throughout the history of redemption.

    b. By drawing attention to himself, Solomon draws attention to the true King of Israel, the Beloved of the Father, and His perfect rule.

3. Solomon was not a perfect king, as clearly seen in God's requirements of the king of Israel in Deuteronomy 17.

    a. Solomon married foreign wives, and his heart was led astray into the false worship of idolatry (1 Kings 11:9).

    b. Solomon amassed for himself great wealth and trusted in horses and chariots rather than in the Lord; this violated God's law.

4. Solomon's failure pointed Israel to the King they would ultimately need, the king whose rightful possession to the throne has been demonstrated in the Gospels—Jesus Christ, the fulfillment of the Psalms.

STUDY QUESTIONS

1. Why are Psalms 113 to 118 called "The Egyptian Hallel"?
   a. Christians sing them to commemorate Israel's history.
   b. Christians sing them to connect with Israel's heritage.
   c. Jews sing them on pilgrimage to Jerusalem.
   d. Jews sing them at the Passover meal.

2. How is Psalm 119 intentionally placed within Book Five of the Psalter?
   a. To balance out the brevity of Psalm 17
   b. To center Book Five as the climatic psalm
   c. To match the chronological features of Book Five
   d. To celebrate the law of God as a reason for praise

3. The argument that Jesus is nowhere explicitly mentioned in the Psalms is a valid argument against exclusive psalmody.
   a. True
   b. False

4. How is Solomon able to point to Christ by placing himself at the center of Psalm 127?
   a. The person of Christ is referenced by the names of Solomon.
   b. The glory of Christ is reflected in the earthly glory of Solomon.
   c. The name of Christ is explicitly stated in the psalms of Solomon.
   d. The faithfulness of Christ is amplified by the faithfulness of Solomon.

5. Which violation of God's law does Solomon commit that seems most to contradict Psalm 127?
   a. Solomon's foreign wives
   b. Solomon's trust in horses
   c. Solomon's wayward heart
   d. Solomon's idolatrous practice

6. Which gospel accounts place the greatest emphasis on the kingship of Jesus Christ?
    a. Matthew and Mark
    b. Luke and John
    c. Matthew and Luke
    d. Mark and John

DISCUSSION QUESTIONS

1. How is Book Five of the Psalter organized in relation to Israel? Has studying the Psalms given you a greater appreciation of Scripture? Why?

2. What are the Psalms of Ascents? Thinking in terms of Lord's Day worship, how can the Psalms of Ascents be applied to your life as a Christian?

3. How are children viewed in the Psalms? What did Dr. Godfrey mean by warning us not to oversentimentalize children by using the psalms?

4. Do you suppose that Solomon wrote Psalm 127 before or after his heart turned away from the Lord? Why? In what way does the glory of Solomon's kingdom and the sin of Solomon's kingdom point to Jesus Christ?

12

Psalm 145: God Is All

INTRODUCTION

The final psalms in the Psalter are the culmination of praise to which the entire book has been leading. In this lesson, Dr. Godfrey closes his survey through the Psalms by taking a closer look at Psalm 145, the last psalm of Book Five.

LESSON OBJECTIVES

1. To argue the case for Psalm 145 as the last psalm of Book Five
2. To examine the structure and exegete the content of Psalm 145
3. To encourage a continued love for the Psalms beyond this study

SCRIPTURE READING

The LORD is gracious and merciful, slow to anger and abounding in steadfast love. The LORD is good to all, and his mercy is over all that he has made.

—Psalm 145:8–9

LECTURE OUTLINE

A. The last five psalms in the Psalter function as conclusions to each of the five books of the Psalter, culminating the entire Psalter in an exaltation of praise.

1. Psalm 145 can be called the last psalm of Book Five because the last five psalms of the Psalter are one unit, each beginning and ending with the refrain, "Praise the LORD!"

2. Psalms 146–150 are individual conclusions to the five books of the Psalter.
   a. Psalm 146 concludes Book One as a praise for God's care.
   b. Psalm 147 concludes Book Two as a praise for God's kingdom.
   c. Psalm 148 concludes Book Three as a praise for God's promises.
   d. Psalm 149 concludes Book Four as a praise for God's faithfulness.
   e. Psalm 150 concludes Book Five as a praise for God's salvation.

B. Psalm 145, an acrostic psalm with a textual variant, brings Book Five to a close.

   1. Psalm 145 is an acrostic psalm, meaning that the lines of the psalm begin with consecutive letters of the Hebrew alphabet.

   2. The Psalter contains nine acrostic psalms; Psalm 119 being the longest and most well known.

   3. Psalm 145:13 contains a bracketed verse that is not found in every Hebrew manuscript (see footnote on v. 13 in the English Standard Version).

      a. The bracketed material in verse 13 corresponds to the Hebrew letter *nun* or *n*.

      b. If the bracketed portion of verse 13 is original to the text, then the entire Hebrew alphabet is represented.

      c. If the bracketed portion of verse 13 is not original to the text, then David is using an artful variation on the alphabetic poetic device.

      d. The bracketed material of verse 13 is likely original if you consider the improbability of a copyist's composing and adding an entire verse.

C. Psalm 145 moves back and forth between praises for God's character and praises for God's works such that the enthusiasm of the psalmist cannot be missed.

   1. Psalm 145:1–3 begins the psalm in praise of God's character, celebrating God's greatness in the knowledge that "His greatness is unsearchable."

   2. Psalm 145:4–6 follows with a praise of God's works, which in the first half of Psalm 145 are not specifically named in order to prompt our meditation.

   3. Psalm 145:7 returns to a praise of God's character, stressing the goodness of God alongside the greatness of His character.

   4. Psalm 145:8 continues to extol the character of God by quoting from a verse at the heart of biblical religion: God's revelation to Moses in Exodus 34:6.

   5. Psalm 145:9 activates the theme of universality by describing the extent of God's mercy and love "over all that he has made."

   6. Psalm 145:11–13 is the center of Psalm 145 and continues the theme of universality by describing God's kingdom as extending to all generations.

   7. Psalm 145:14–16 draws our attention to specific works of God.

      a. God is a merciful God, willing to condescend to us in our need, as seen in Psalm 145:14 and enumerated upon in Psalm 111.

      b. God is a provisional God, able to supply His people in abundance, as seen in Psalm 145:15–16.

   8. Psalm 145:17–18 remarks on the character behind God's works, reminding us through the struggles of life that God is a kind God who is near to us.

   9. Psalm 145:19–20 contrast God's love for those who call upon Him with the sure condemnation that awaits the wicked who refuse to be saved.

  10. Psalm 145:21 concludes Psalm 145 in a most fitting and appropriate way.

      a. Psalm 145:21 unites the personal and communal aspects of biblical religion: "*My mouth* will speak . . . and let *all flesh* bless his holy name."

      b. Psalm 145:21 concludes Book Five of the Psalter in accordance with the purpose of the Psalter: "Praise the Lord!"

D. Throughout this series, we have learned to love the poetic beauty and rich praises found throughout the Psalms, so now we must continue to love the Psalms.

　　1. Every effort you invest into learning the Psalms will be richly rewarded, so continue to read and familiarize yourself with them.

　　2. Singing the Psalms is a great way to learn the Psalter, so continue to read and familiarize yourself with them expressively and musically.

　　3. Encourage your church to have a class or series on the Psalms, so that you may continue to be enriched in your knowledge of God's truths.

STUDY QUESTIONS

1. What do the last five psalms of the Psalter have in common with the first two psalms of the Psalter?
    a. They are centered on the person and work of Christ.
    b. They each relate to the five books of the Psalter.
    c. They all begin and end with "Praise the Lord."
    d. They are not ascribed a particular author.

2. If Psalm 148 is a praise of the promises of God, then to what book of the Psalter does it correspond?
    a. Book One
    b. Book Two
    c. Book Three
    d. Book Four

3. Psalm 145 moves back and forth between God's character and God's works by praising God's works before God's character.
    a. True
    b. False

4. What is an argument for maintaining the entire Hebrew alphabet in the original text of Psalm 145?
    a. Allowing for copyist error undermines faith in Scripture's inspiration.
    b. Missing letters in an alphabetical poem seems nonsensical.
    c. Important doctrinal points would be lost from the psalm.
    d. Copyists did not typically add entire lines to a text.

5. What is the most famous acrostic psalm in the Psalter?
    a. Psalm 111
    b. Psalm 112
    c. Psalm 119
    d. Psalm 145

6. Psalm 145 concludes with which of the following?
   a. A celebration of the universality of God's love to future generations
   b. A proclamation of the greatness of God's character
   c. A promise from the psalmist to praise the Lord
   d. A warning to the wicked to repent

DISCUSSION QUESTIONS

1. Explain Dr. Godfrey's argument for Psalm 145 being the last psalm in Book Five of the Psalter. Are you convinced of his argument? Why?

2. How did you react to Dr. Godfrey's discussion of the manuscript evidence issues of Psalm 145? Why should you still be confident that the Bible is trustworthy?

3. How is Christianity's emphasis on God's goodness different from other world religions? How is God's steadfast love and mercy at the heart of biblical religion?

4. What measures will you take after the completion of this study to continue loving the Psalms?

ANSWER KEY FOR STUDY QUESTIONS

Lesson 1
1. B
2. B
3. C
4. B
5. B
6. C

Lesson 2
1. D
2. C
3. B
4. C
5. C
6. B

Lesson 3
1. C
2. B
3. B
4. D
5. B
6. B

Lesson 4
1. C
2. D
3. B
4. D
5. C
6. C

Lesson 5
1. D
2. C
3. B
4. D
5. A
6. D

Lesson 6
1. C
2. A
3. A
4. D
5. D
6. B

Lesson 7
1. B
2. A
3. A
4. C
5. C
6. B

Lesson 8
1. D
2. B
3. B
4. D
5. C
6. B

Lesson 9
1. A
2. B
3. B
4. D
5. A
6. D

Lesson 10
1. D
2. C
3. B
4. D
5. D
6. C

Lesson 11
1. D
2. C
3. B
4. B
5. B
6. C

Lesson 12
1. D
2. C
3. B
4. D
5. C
6. C